Written by David Yale

Illustrated by US Illustrations

2025

First printing, 2025.

To my kids, Griffin, Jared and Cameron,
for bringing out the kid in me...

"OK Mikey, Mommy and Daddy said it's time for bed."

"One more? Please Poppy."

"OK Mikey, one more. Just one."

"And the Bobcats win!"

“One more?”

"We just did one more, you silly! It's time..."

"Time to brush our teeth."

"Brush and brush, those bristles never seem to stop working..."

"Brush and brush, you'll make your teeth so very clean..."

"So brush and brush, the cleanest teeth you've ever seen."

"Now rinse, and rinse..."

"Your dentist will be so happy..."

"Cause far and wide as he can see..."

"Not even a single cavity!"

After all that singing, maybe Poppy is ready to go beddy bye too!

The End

www.ingramcontent.com/pod-product-compliance
Lightning Source LLC
LaVergne TN
LVHW070202110826
845147LV00002B/474
* 9 7 9 8 9 9 8 5 2 7 1 6 6 *